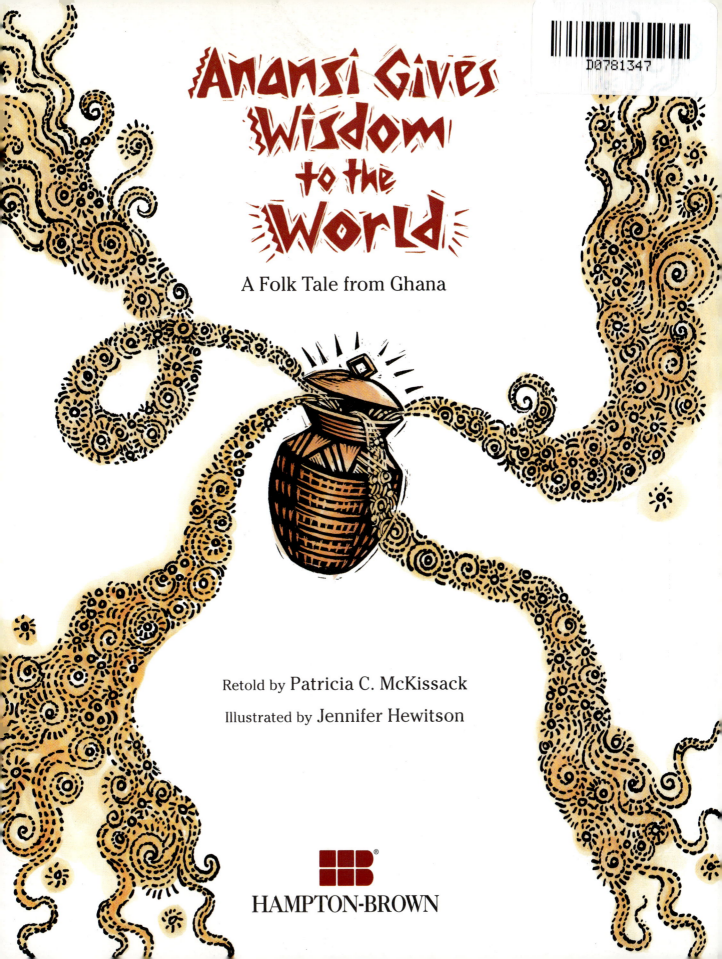

Anansi Gives Wisdom to the World

A Folk Tale from Ghana

Retold by Patricia C. McKissack

Illustrated by Jennifer Hewitson

HAMPTON-BROWN

Characters

Anansi

Anansi's son

Anansi has a pot of wisdom. What will he do with it?

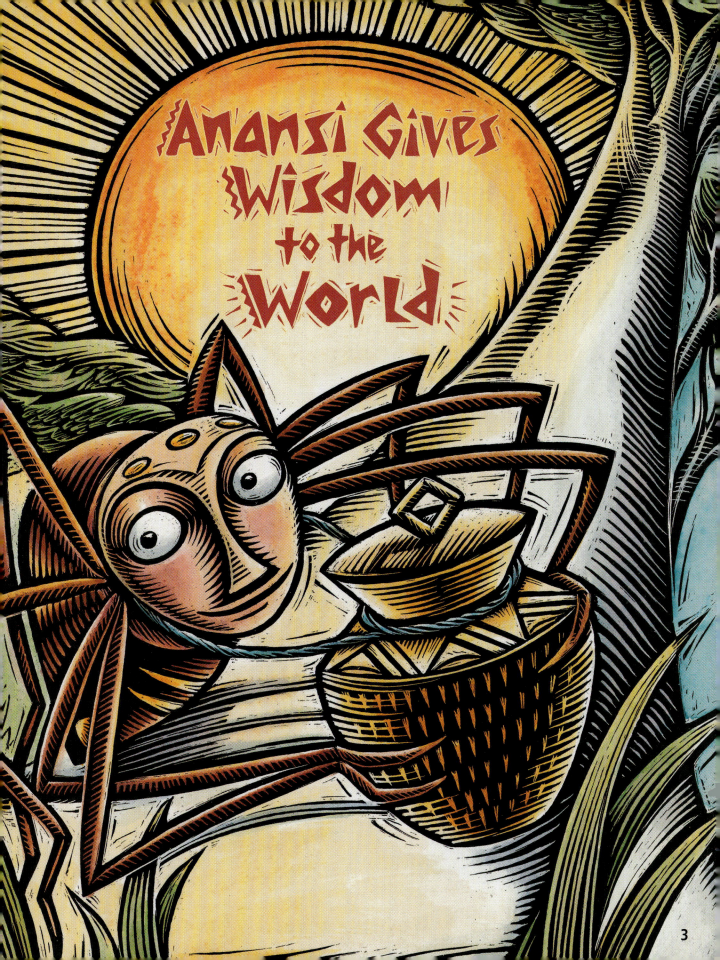

A story, a story! This is a story about Anansi the spider. Anansi thinks he is wise, but he isn't.

One day, Nyame the Sky God visits Anansi.

"I have a gift for you," Nyame says. "Here is all the wisdom in the world. Share this wisdom with everyone!"

Anansi does not share. He wants
all the wisdom for himself!

Anansi hides the wisdom in a pot.
Then he covers the pot.

Anansi ties the pot around his neck.
He opens the pot and peeks into it again
and again. The wisdom is still there!

Anansi crawls away from the other animals. He does not want them to see his pot.

Anansi is happy. He has all the wisdom in the world! Anansi laughs. He dances, and he sings.

All for Me

Chant

I take the wisdom of the world
And hide it all away.
I put it in this little pot.
I carry it all day.
  Me, me! Mine, mine!

I keep the wisdom of the world.
I keep it all for me.
I want to be the wise one,
As wise as wise can be.
  Me, me! Mine, mine!

Anansi loves his wisdom. But he thinks, "Someone might steal the pot!"

He looks left and right. He looks up and down. He looks all around. Then he spots a tall, tall tree.

"I can hide my wisdom up there," Anansi says.

Anansi picks up the pot and crawls over to the tree. He steps onto the trunk.

One leg goes up. Two legs go up. Three legs go up . . .

Then Anansi slips! He falls down to the ground.

SMACK! He hits his head hard!

Anansi tries again. One leg goes up. Two legs go up . . .

He slides and drops. He trips and tumbles. The tired spider climbs all day and all night, but he falls down each time.

Anansi's friends watch him. They know he is a good climber. They wonder why he falls.

The Problem

Anansi climbs. *(clap, clap)*

Anansi crawls. *(stomp, stomp)*

Anansi slips, *(clap, clap)*

And then he falls! *(stomp, stomp)*

What's the problem, Anansi?

Anansi climbs, *(clap, clap)*

And slides back down. *(stomp, stomp)*

Anansi drops, *(clap, clap)*

And hits the ground! *(stomp, stomp)*

What's the problem, Anansi?

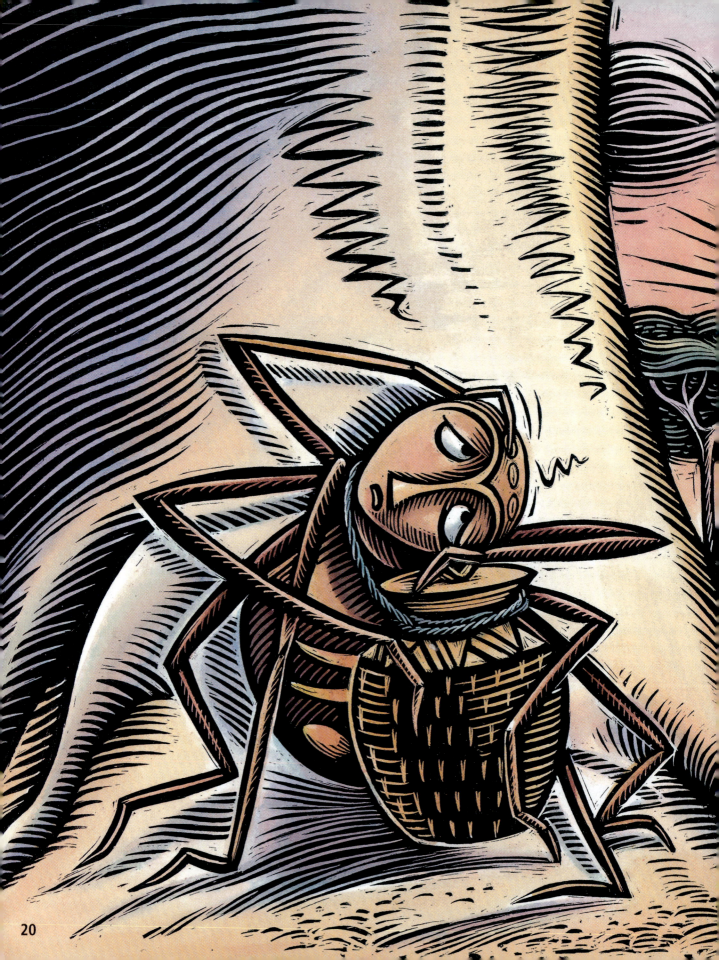

"I know what the problem is!" says a little voice. The voice comes from Anansi's son.

"Father," the little spider says, "the pot hangs in front of you. Your legs hit it, and you slip. Put the pot on your back and then climb."

Anansi moves the pot to his back. He begins to climb.

One leg goes up. Two legs go up. Three legs go up. Four legs go up . . .

Anansi climbs up and up. He does not fall!

He climbs all the way to the top of the tall tree!

Anansi sits at the top and smiles.
Then he frowns.
"I have all this wisdom," he says,
"but my little son still has more wisdom
than I do!"
Anansi is unhappy.

Anansi gets angrier and angrier.
Finally, he throws the pot of wisdom
out of the tree.

The pot falls to the ground and breaks.

Pieces of wisdom fly everywhere.

People all over the earth pick up the
pieces. Now the whole world has wisdom!

Wisdom

I have wisdom.
You have it, too.
Every woman has wisdom.
Every man has it, too!

All the children have wisdom.
They have a lot.
We all have wisdom
From Anansi's pot!

Anansi's story teaches us this wise saying:
"No person has all the wisdom. But everyone
has some of it."